*The Point*

# The Point

---

Sherry McRae Sims

Charleston, SC
www.PalmettoPublishing.com

*The Point*

Copyright © 2023 by Sherry McRae Sims

All rights reserved

No portion of this book may be reproduced, stored in a retrieval system, or transmitted in any form by any means–electronic, mechanical, photocopy, recording, or other–except for brief quotations in printed reviews, without prior permission of the author.

First Edition

Paperback ISBN: 979-8-8229-2031-6
eBook ISBN: 979-8-8229-2032-3

Dedicated to God, His Son,
and the Holy Spirit

"What We Become"
by Hastings W. Coach (May 5, 2022)

Although we may be born into what shapes us
It's what we learn to accept or reject that makes us
Either way, Our creator never leaves or forsakes us

Pull back when unfounded doubt turns into fear that threatens to become self-hate
Never allow constant inner conflict to become your fate

Childhood's fairy tale endings were only an illusion
This sphere on which we dwell is no more than a ball of confusion

We contemplate priorities and what comes first, chicken or egg
Past indiscretions still haunt like a plaque
Your next "bad choice" can be the one that drives you to your grave
We lie, cheat, or steal as if these vices are shackled to our leg
As for mercy and forgiveness, we're too proud to beg

Never allow fear induced hatred to become rage
Only constant prayer and meditation can return that animal to its cage

Let's not be loath to confront what unrequited love becomes in its desperate dying stage
Let's hope that discerning between what we can change and what we accept doesn't come at too high a wage

Let's hope that the wisdom to know the difference comes with age
Acknowledge when a chapter in your life is over, and gracefully turn the page
These lessons may not be taught in the standard curriculum at school
Just heed Grandmom's warning " Ain't nothin like an ole fool"

With no way to know how much hardship we'll endure or when this life will be done
When the grim reaper knocks, we'll all someday succumb
I want to be one who rests in the comfort, I became all that God wanted me to become

# The Point

I was born on September 11, 1954. I would not know I was different until later on. I was given away shortly after birth to my adopted parents, Harry and Mary Commedore.

One of the main points of this story is that God let me (Sherry) live and not be aborted. As you will see, God played an important part in my life from the beginning until now. My adopted mom, Mary, raised me in the African Methodist Episcopal (AME) Church. I was as good as I could be because back then, punishments meant whippings with a switch or beatings with a belt. As time went on, Mary and Harry adopted another child, who was my brother, James. James was very rebellious and got many whippings. James liked to tease me and get me upset. My mom said he had the devil in him, and she tried to beat the devil out of him.

When I was about five years old, my dad taught me how to print my name. I can remember that my dad was an inspiration to me. I used to sit on his knee and learn. He had dark skin, almost as dark as chocolate. Near the end of his life, he taught me a song. He laid in bed and sang to me. The song was, "Lead Me, Guide Me Along The Way," for if you lead me, I cannot stray. Lord, let me walk each day with thee; lead me, oh, Lord, lead me.

I wrote this poem for him.

Daddy, I missed you when you went away,
I didn't even see your hair turn gray,
My dad, I cry when I think of you and your loving ways.
How great it would be if you could join me in my days.

Every tear I shed is a piece of my heart.
It forms the word "love" when broken apart
The days you held me on your knee
I wish my dad I could see

I miss your tender hand
You were such a godly man
You took your hand and placed it on mine
You showed me how to write each line

Daddy, I miss your kind, sweet spirit
If only you could hear me sing
There is a sweet peace in my soul because of you,
Daddy I love you and always will
I'm saying I miss you
Love from a broken-hearted little girl

When Mom told me my daddy died, I was angry. I thought the doctors could make anyone better. Why did God take my dad from me? I knew about heaven, but I thought only old people went there.

Now it is time to tell you about my mom, Mary. I will just call her mom. She has been my mom since a few days after my birth. She was an amazing woman. I don't know where I would be if it had not been for her. What was so special about this woman of God? She only had a ninth-grade education. She taught herself to read and write, yet she taught me to love the Lord. I can remember one of the first songs she taught me, "Jesus Loves Me." She had me baptized in the AME church as a toddler. Her love fueled my love of Jesus. She showed, by example, how to worship God. Not only did she take me to church, but she went too.

I always wanted to be an angel, so I acted really well at church; I did not want to go to hell. My mom always told us the devil was a liar, and no matter what we did, we would not get punished if we told the truth. I got whippings, but not as many as my brother. After my dad passed, my mom took over as breadwinner. There was never a day when we were hungry. She later told someone that when there was just enough for us, she would wipe her mouth with a greasy napkin and pretend she had already eaten. I know it was hard for my mom, a colored women, as we were called at the time, to raise two children on her own.

I can remember waking up in the middle of the night and hearing my mom singing a song and cleaning.

I would say, "Mommy, why are you up?"

She would say, " I was talking to the Lord. I couldn't sleep, so I did a little cleaning." She also said, "An idle mind is the devil's workshop," so she kept busy while she was up.

Perhaps that's where I got my love of singing and praying—from her and my dad. The love of learning did not rub off so much. Mom studied and took classes to be a licensed practical nurse. At that time, they did not need a license. She got her training, was able to quit cleaning houses, and did private duty nursing.

I got really nervous after my dad passed. I had a lot of pressure for an eight-year-old. I had to cook, clean, and watch my brother while my mom worked. My mom noticed that I was not myself. She talked to me and said she would take me to a doctor, whom she worked for, to see if he could help me. He was a surgeon, but a very wise man. He knew I had some problems. It was almost unheard of for children to have mental illness at that time, in the early sixties. It was a mental illness. The doctor gave me Librium and told my mom how to give it to me. My brother teased me a lot because I was trying to be a mom, but it did not work out so well.

I can recall one time when my mom was at work and my brother set the house on fire. The fire chief asked him if he did it. At first, he said no. After the chief told him he would go to jail if he started a fire, my brother admitted to it. I am sure he told them he was playing with matches and didn't mean to do it. He did not go to jail this time. His constant teasing and getting into trouble took their toll on me. I wrote this poem about mental illness.

I think I hear them talking about me
I think I'm lost in my own head
You see, I hear scary sounds in the air
I stand alone in fear

I feel my face change with each thought
Negativity is overpowering me
Nasty thoughts come into my head
I cannot sleep in my own bed
Please tell me this is just a dream
It's mental illness, and she's queen

She is wicked, unkind, and full of bull
She makes me wish I could die
She has even given me ways to say,
"You are rotten and no good like hell"
There is no escape
Can't you tell?

But I've found a way to beat it
It's Jesus, and he is King!

I went home, but over time, the illness did not improve. My mom sent me away to her brother and his wife's in Baltimore to stay for one year in hopes I would get better. This worked! After one year, I was ready to face the world again, if it had not been for an incident there.

One day early on, I was outside. I thought the moon was falling from the sky. I screamed, "It's the end of the world." I knew my aunt was shocked.

She took me inside and said the end of the world would not come right now, and it would be a long time before it would come. She told me never to shout like that again. I never did during the year I stayed with her. Finally, the year came to an end, and I went back to my mom, Mary. I was so happy to return; it was the longest year of my life.

Years went by like leaves falling. My brother had many behavioral problems. He had so many issues that my mom took him to a hypnotist. He also went to a psychologist. I wanted attention too, so I asked if I should go too. My mom let me attend a session. I said maybe it would help me improve my grades. My grades stayed pretty much the same after my meeting with the hypnotist. As time went by, I had bouts of depression, but they always passed with prayer and time. At age eighteen, I graduated from McKeesport Senior High School. My mom was so proud of me that at the graduation, she shouted, "Praise the Lord." It was an extra special moment for her since a lot of people of color did not finish high school—including her and my dad. It was an accomplishment.

In addition to graduating, I found my sweetheart, John McRae. He was handsome and suave. I didn't really want to get married so soon, but my mom made me promise that if I followed John back to Washington, DC, we would not live in sin. In other words, I was pressured to marry him. Since I tried to do everything to please her, I joined him in holy matrimony. Little did I know that it was the beginning of my mental illness becoming full blown. I was in shock when I arrived in the DC area. I had to grow up fast. There were so many people of different ethnic groups and cultures. My eyes were opened. I met people from all over the world. I even met a princess from Africa. How amazing this was to me! DC was so fast that it was like being in another world. Everyone was going so fast that it seemed as if they didn't bother to speak. It was like seeing cattle in a fast-moving herd. If you didn't get out of the way, they would knock you down.

There was a subway that I had never ridden on. I soon learned to ride the subway and navigate my way around, even riding in a taxi when I got lost. I could get to DC in a flash. My first job was with a temp agency. Through my time with the temp agency, I got a job with the US Railroad. The government contracted with us for ten thousand dollars from the temp agency because of the great reputation we had with them. I was so excited that I could not believe it. My first, good-paying job with benefits and the opportunity to ride the railroad for free for the rest of my life. I could hardly believe it! I was a young woman from McKeesport, Pennsylvania, with such a prestigious position. Even today, I never got that offer again. I only worked at the railroad for a short time because my illness had come full circle.

I was on the way home from work on the subway when I thought I heard voices of people on the train talking negatively about me. They were saying things like, "She's crazy. She can't even hold herself together. Her face is changing to that of an older woman. That must be her mom. She really is sick. We don't need her here. Send her dumb ass back to PA."

I was in the early stages of paranoia. I was afraid and kept hearing voices. I made it home. I even thought that the people who took care of my children were laughing and talking about me. I thought if I could make it home, the voices would go away. I made my way home, but the voices never stopped. They kept getting worse. I could hear voices from inside my apartment saying, "She's no good. She is a bad person. She can't even take care of her children."

I could not even watch television. The voices were coming through the television. I knew I was going out of my mind. I call this being on broadcast when you hear things through the radio, TV, or the walls. This is not the professional term for it. I use it to refer to my own symptoms. I was so out of it after I put the children to bed. It got worse. I had a Mickey Mouse doll, and I thought it was staring at me, so I burned the doll in the garbage room. I heard what I thought was the devil talking to me. Of course, he was not nice.

This went on and lasted so long that I couldn't even go to work. I lost my good job. I never called in to say I was sick. I covered my ears, sat on the couch, and tried to make the voices stop. When my husband realized I could not take care of the children or myself, he called my mom in Pennsylvania. She told him to bring me there, and she would get help for me. By the time we gotten to Pennsylvania, things had deteriorated even more. I would not eat because I thought my mom and John were trying to poison me. Finally, they took me to McKeesport Hospital. I had lost weight because I would not eat. I passed out in the ER. I must have been combative because when I woke up, I was restrained. My arms and legs were held tightly by leather straps. I tried to escape. Guess what? I did escape! I was so thin that I worked my wrist and legs out of the leather straps, and I jumped over the stretcher and ran down the hall. 'Wouldn't you know that I would get caught?

I ran right into the biggest white security guard I ever saw. Needless to say, I ran back to the room, jumped over the side of the stretcher, and laid back down. After being strapped back in bed, I decided that since I could not escape at this time and they were all evil people, I would sing my way out. God would hear me and send angels to rescue me. I sang every song I knew, and that lasted for a long time. I knew a lot of songs since I was raised in the church and attended every Sunday.

As I write this, tears come to my eyes because it was pitiful. I can relive the moments of this nightmare. After causing so much commotion, they must have given me more medication because I remember waking up again; this time, I knew I was in heaven. Yes, I believed I had died and was in heaven. All around me were people in white. I thought they were angels, preparing me to see God. They were nurses and a psychiatrist. The doctor asked me if I knew what day it was. I don't remember what day I said it was, but it was the wrong answer. Then he also asked if I knew where I was. I answered wrong, and again I said heaven. I believe he asked me one more question. All I know is that I didn't answer that right. He told me they were going to have to admit me to the psychiatric ward. This is not what I expected; this is not the way to heaven. I believe he left the room, and I fell asleep again. When I woke up this time I was in a wheelchair. I was so disappointed because I did not see God. I imagined I had died, but I was in hell because I did not make it to heaven. I was willing to wait until I could make it to heaven, so I just kept my eyes closed as long as I could. I did not speak. I heard people talking to me, but I did not respond.

Every day would go by, and I still would not speak. I had my menstrual cycle, and the nurses and staff had to change my sanitary pads. My mom, Mary, and my husband came to see me. They talked to me, but I didn't answer. I believe that since God did not show up, I was not allowed to speak until He showed up. I was even fed by the staff. I did not even respond to the simple things they asked me to do. I thought this was my punishment for not being good enough to see God. I was alive but in a semi-coma state. I heard the doctor say they were going to give me electric shock therapy. I thought, "Oh boy, now, God is really going to torture me." My family agreed to give me shock treatments.

At this point, I could not speak. So twice a week, I got electroconvulsive shock therapy (ECT), and I was also given 500 mg of Thorazine twice a day, which was a very strong dose, but I was very depressed. At the end of thirty days of treatment, I heard them say they were going to put me away in a state hospital. I had six ECT treatments. It was the most they could give me.

My family seemed very sad that they were going to have to put me away. The next day, after completing the shock therapy treatment, something very strange happened. I felt as though I was floating above myself. I could see myself sitting there. I looked down at myself and thought I must be dreaming. What I had was an out-of-body experience. I was looking at myself sitting in the wheelchair when I heard a soft, sweet voice. This is what I remember.

The voice said, "Sherry, do you want to just sit there forever, or do you want to get on with your life?"

I pondered for a minute. I said, "I want to get on with my life." Well, get up, speak, and do it. I believe this gave me permission to finally speak again.

When my husband and mom came the next day, my husband asked my mom if he could try something. My husband began to sing, "Thank God for You, Baby." It was a popular song in the 1970s. I started to sing with him.

My mom was so elated that she said, "Praise the Lord."

They started to talk to me, and I responded just in the nick of time. My thirty days had expired. Everyone was pleased. I was happy too. I would not be taken to a state hospital. I stayed a few more days, and Dr. Brink planned my release. The stipulations were that I would take 500 mg of Thorazine twice a day and come back once a month to be evaluated. He told us that as long as I rested and followed directions, I could be weaned off the medication by the end of the year. I had the best psychiatrist. Dr. Brink was the Chief of Psychiatry. He knew how to treat me. At the sessions, Dr. Brink asked me how I was feeling, and if my ideations had improved. Each time, I progressed. I was soon ready to rejoin the real world.

In 1975, I became pregnant with our first child. I was still with my husband, John. This is proof that God does not give us what we ask for if it is not His will. We were afraid we could not have children, and God allowed us to have them. We were thinking about adoption. I had a baby girl in August 1976. I enjoyed being a mom. I was very busy. I had to work and take care of my child. There was one problem. I got the mother's blues—postpartum depression. After the birth of a child, some women suffer from it. It can go away, but my blues lingered. I tried to be happy, but it did not work. I became unable to work. I told my ob-gyn doctor about it, and he said it would go away. I started to hear voices again and was afraid to go outside. Mental illness showed its ugly face again.

\* \* \*

One day, I got into a fight with John. After arguing with him, I chose to believe it was the end of the world. I told John that God was coming to take me with him. I yelled at John, and he yelled back at me. I told him the Lord was coming that night. I shouted, "Here he comes knocking at the door," in a song-like tune. John was so shocked when a loud knock came at the door. I was surprised God had shown. He was right on time. I thought, "I won't let John open the door." I blocked the door. John shoved me out of the way. John had called the EMTs to take me to the hospital.

They talked really nice to me, and I was assuming they would take me to see God. One of the EMTs said, "We are going to take you to the hospital to get checked out." They told me to get on the stretcher.

I refused. I told them I would walk. In the dead of winter with at least two inches of snow, I walked to the ambulance with no shoes on. I was shouting, "Don't you hurt God's angel." I was going somewhere, but it was not to heaven.

I was taken to the behavioral health or psychiatric ward. Meanwhile, John took my baby to my in-laws. I was being prepared for Jesus, so I thought, so I acted nice. A man in a white coat and the nurses, who I thought were angels, asked me, "Do you know what day and year it is?" I said the wrong day and the wrong year. I failed the first test. They continued to ask questions. None of my answers made any sense at all.

"Do you know where you are?"

I said, "I'm in heaven." Well, it was bad enough that I didn't know the day or year. But I didn't even know where I was.

They told me you are in Prince George's Hospital Psych Ward, and we are going to admit you.

I think I said, "Are you crazy? I have a date with Jesus." I was tired and probably fell asleep.

When I woke up, I was restrained in bed. I was probably fighting because I believed they were going to hurt me. I got more out of control, and this time when I woke up, I was in a padded room on a mattress on the floor. I had a straitjacket on. It held my arms in place, so I could not hurt myself or anyone else. My food was served through a window in the door on a paper tray with plastic silverware. I had lost so much weight that I did a Houdini and escaped out of the straight jacket. I still could not get out of the room. I stayed there until I promised not to hurt anyone or act out. I was still very sick, but they let me return to my room.

\* \* \*

It was Christmas, and we were decorating the hospital room doors. We won first place, even with little help from me, because my roommate was very artistic. I'm not sure what we won—maybe an extra coffee or a ribbon; I can't remember. I still thought Jesus was coming for me, so I walked up and down the halls, reading the Bible. The nurse told me I would have to stop because it was scaring the other residents. I still sat quietly and read to myself.

I met a foot doctor named Dr. Tatter. He volunteered to take care of the patients' feet. He took me into the room where he was assigned to see patients and treat my feet. We talked. I was so impressed by him. He was Jewish and had knowledge of the Bible. I told him that one day Jesus would come and there would be new heavens and earth where we could live in peace.

I also told him I was an earth angel. I said, "God told me when the new Bible was written, he would be in it." I wrote a poem for him after we talked. Writing was one of the gifts I received from God. I asked Him one day before this encounter with Dr. Tatter, "What was my talent?" I did not have any. He told me I could write because the Holy Spirit would help me. That was back in the early 1970s, and I am still writing today. The poem I wrote for Dr. Tatter is in two parts. Here it is. I wrote it while I was still pretty ill.

### Poem for Dr. Tattar, Part I

Sitting down I tried to write as hard as I could with all my might.
A lovely poem for a beautiful person who is truly out of sight.
Most doctors depersonalize you playing the money game.
You are in a class by yourself, you are not the same.
You remember my face and know my name.
Good vibes radiate from you, being a friend is nothing new.
You work with feet and bones, that's just half the story.
Your heart is filled with love and blooms like a morning glory.

## Part II

I'm not sure what to say to you.
You are not really given credit for what you do.
So thankful for the privilege of knowing someone
as sensitive and kind as you.
Whether or not you are praised by many or few,
I must give credit where it is due.
So much love and compassion is gone these days,
it is good to see someone who possesses those ways

I suffered as a result of mental illness. I felt at times like I was in heaven in God's presence. Then, some days, I was in hell. I could not stay in balance. After getting out of the hospital, I started my life again, but not right away. I had to take medication and go to therapy every month. My medications were monitored and changed as I improved. If you think this is the end, it is not. This is why the book is called The Point. The Father, Son, and Holy Spirit make up the point. Also, the three rivers in Pittsburgh meet at the point. The Pittsburgh area is where I grew up. The point is a special area because it reminds me of God's power to bring three rivers together. Father, Jesus, and the Holy Spirit are the keys to my life. Through it all, God was with me. I could not have made it without Him. Mental illness is not to be laughed at. It affects people in many different ways. I am not an expert. I can only tell you what I've been through.

My minister, Reverend Dr. Lora Adams-King, said, "You don't look like what you've been through," and I don't think I do.

Please help those suffering from mental illness and depression. There are many forms of it. I can't name them all. I just know it is a disease like cancer or diabetes and can affect anyone. Some people live with it or survive with it, and some suffer in silence. I just came out there with my illness recently. It is time for people to know about it. I will no longer try to hide it. I am not ashamed anymore. If you need help, tell someone. If someone needs help, please try to get them the help they need. We need to let people know it is okay to ask for help. Help someone today in Jesus's name. I pray for all who are sick and suffering from mental illness. I know I can't be cured, but I can be treated and try to live as normally as possible with God's help, which is the point in my life. Amen.

The following pages have two poems that I wrote on my journey through life. They are written at different times when I was going through my life's struggle with mental illness. It was and is the first book I have ever written. I hope you enjoy them. Remember this was written in the past while I was going through life. I've also written many poems for people who have inspired me in my life. I wish I could have copies of each one, but they know who they are. God gave me the gift of writing, comedy making people laugh, encouragement writing songs, singing, writing children's books. And most of all prayer and praise. I can't list everything, but He has truly blessed me. Just to think I thought I had no talent. Thank you, Lord.

"Jesus"

Jesus is in my car.
Yes, I say Jesus is in my car.
If I am crazy, so are you.
I make room for Him, and if He wants to sit, He does,
If not, He stands or floats in midair.
Ha! You say you've lost your mind?
No, I say I may have lost something, but it's not my mind.
Jesus told me I would not lose it again, and
I have His company whenever I need it.
What do you have?
I have a father, a friend, a companion and more.
What, I say, do you have?

## "Jesus Is in My Car" Part 2

That was in the 1990s, and this is now
And Jesus is still riding in my car.
He puts His foot on the pedal when I need to step on the gas.
He brakes for me until the danger has passed.
He moves all animals out of my way
He sends his angels to protect me when I pray
I give Him full control
He steers the car when I zone out
It is amazing the things He can do
That is why I know He is in control of my car and my soul.

# The Road to Arizona

I am an avid Bible reader. I am just in love with the Lord. I was baptized in the A.M.E. Church as a little girl. I am now a member of New Life Family Worship Center in Franklin, Pennsylvania. Never say to our Father in Heaven, "Here I am. Send me." If you don't mean it, don't say it, because He will send you! One Sunday at our church, Alan McKain spoke about the American Indian Christian Mission (AICM) School in Show Low, Arizona, where he and his wife Melody work. He told of an opening for house parents at the school.

My mission really started after I, Sherry Sims, graduated from Clarion University of Pennsylvania at age forty-nine with a certification as a certified massage therapist (CM.T). I quit my job at Youth Alternatives in Oil City, Pennsylvania, on August 25, 2004, and went on my mission to accept the job in Arizona. I decided that this was where God was leading me. First, I had to convince myself and then my husband, Kenny. I call him "Bear," which is my Native American nickname for him. The first words out of his mouth were, "Woman, you are crazy!" Some of my friends weren't sure that we should go to Arizona. I knew I was doing the right thing. We said our goodbyes, got the addresses of our friends, and most importantly, talked with my adopted mom, Ruth, who sent angels to charge over us on our way to Arizona. After getting Ruth's blessing, we left Franklin in our 2000 Toyota Echo.

One night we ran out of money, so we slept in our car at a Love's Truck Stop. The next day, we went on our way again. We arrived pretty much unscathed in Show Low, Arizona, on September 3, 2004. We stopped at a Kentucky Fried Chicken for something to eat and set foot at the AICM at 12 a.m. midnight.

On September 7, 2004, my husband's illness began to surface. He has a heart condition, and he's diabetic. We needed to find a medical clinic where we could get an appointment quickly and one that would treat Kenny without immediate payment. Alan McKain, the principal at the mission school, recommended a clinic we could go to. When we arrived at the clinic, we were greeted by a man of God, Carter, a physician's assistant (PA). He saw Kenny's condition, took blood tests, and as a result of the blood work, the PA reduced some of Kenny's medications. He told us both to drink more water because we were getting dehydrated.

My husband has Native American roots—Kenny is Blackfoot. I have African American Ancestry. We enjoyed our time with the Native American boys and girls. We were houseparents for sixteen boys in the older boys' dorm. The children at the school are mostly Apache and Navajo. We were beginning to bond with them—they wanted to call us grandpa and grandma in their native language. We told them they were not allowed. They then asked to call us Mom and Dad. We explained that the school rule is not to refer to staff as family; they should call staff members Miss, Mr., or Mrs.

A normal day would begin with us waking up at 5:00 a.m., and then waking up the students at 6:00 a.m. They took turns going to the shower, making their beds, and straightening their sleeping areas. We decided to give prizes for the three neatest sleeping areas as incentives for them. Each boy was assigned chores to do before breakfast, followed by morning devotions and prayer. Then we would walk over to the cafeteria on campus for breakfast. After breakfast, the students went to the gym for exercise before going to school in another building. Groups of students are always accompanied by staff members when going from place to place at the school. After exercise time, we would walk with the boys to the next building for classes.

While the boys were in school, I had some free time. I was in charge of laundry for all the students—socks, underwear, shirts, pants, dresses, sheets, blankets, and pillowcases, plus our personal laundry. Laundry was done every day except Friday, when the students went home, took their clothes with them, and hopefully brought the clothes back clean. After classes, the boys returned to the dorm accompanied by a staff member. They had homework to do and received assistance from the staff as needed. Afterward, it was time to go to the cafeteria for supper. After supper, if their homework is done, the boys have free time to swim, hike, go to the playground, and ride bikes with staff supervision. As the day concluded, the boys would talk to us about their life on the "res" and how they lived. I learned one word in Navajo, hogan, which means house.

I thought we had the perfect job—everything seemed to be going as planned, but God told me not to change the time on my car clock. I didn't know why. God gives clear messages, and they are meant to be obeyed. My husband's health got worse over the next few days. Back to the clinic we went. He couldn't stay awake and had a hard time breathing. The PA told me to look inside Kenny's throat at the uvula. The PA thought Kenny had an allergic reaction, told him to lie down, and proceeded to treat him. His condition worsened so rapidly that I couldn't hardly believe it. I knew he was at death's door. I went to the car to call a friend. I cried on the phone for about two minutes until I could speak.

My best friend, Janis, said, "Sherry, is that you?"

Finally, I could answer. I said, "Kenny is dying."

"What?" she said in shock.

I said, "Kenny is dying. I don't want him to die here." I knew the devil was angry because we obeyed God's request by going on the mission. Later, I learned that Kenny had a visit from his mom, who had passed away twenty years ago. When she walked into the clinic, a bright light came before her entrance.

When she walked in, Ken said, "What's up?"

She had long black hair and was beautiful. She looked like an angel. She said to him, "You are not ready to leave earth yet."

Kenny was so ill that I said many fast prayers. I asked God to let Kenny live and to take me instead. I was really afraid because I knew He had the power to do that. I went to the mission with a note from the PA that explained Kenny's grave condition. I cried hard with the administrator and his assistant, Alan. I decided that if anything happened to Kenny, I would drive the car over the Grand Canyon to see if it could fly. Afterward, I did not think either idea was good.

Finally, Kenny was alert enough to go home to the mission. The students kept asking how Mr. Sims was doing. During the night, the PA kept calling and had me check Kenny's respirations and pulse. He remained stable. With everything that had happened, I had not taken my own medicine because I did not have enough money for it. I didn't realize that with all the stress, I was ill too. I was retaining fluid and emotionally breaking down. The next morning, we went back to the clinic and returned the oxygen tank because Kenny didn't believe that he was really sick. I asked the PA to explain to Kenny that I thought he was going to die there.

The PA said, "He's not going to die in my office." He told Kenny that he had developed pneumonia and that the high altitude was making it more difficult for him to breathe. We were advised to get back to Pennsylvania ASAP. We went back to AICM and packed as fast as we could, just throwing things into the car. My birthday is on September 11, and the houseparents and teachers planned a party and baked a cake for me. We were leaving on September 10th, so I didn't get to eat any of my cake. They told me later that they ate it without me.

Little miracles began to happen. A man from the school asked me when we were leaving. He said, "Sherry, God told me to give this to you." He handed me $50.00.

I told Kenny, "God sent me $50.00 for my 50th birthday." Roger, the administrator, also gave us $200.00 to help us on our way back to Pennsylvania. We finished packing, left AICM, and stopped in New Mexico at a hotel that night. The next morning, we arose early, and after eating, we were on our way again. Our next stop would be Texas. We were so glad to get to Texas because of the lower altitude, which would be better for Kenny. When we saw a Walmart, I told Kenny to stop so I could spend my birthday gift from God.

I bought two hats, a blouse, and a skirt. I traveled on to Oklahoma, where I could not believe the rest area had a hole for the restroom toilet. I was getting mentally drained. I fell on the ground, laughing. A lady came over to me and asked what was wrong? I said it was a hole inside for the bathroom. She said there are still outside bathrooms in Ukraine. I said I was sorry, but it was 2004, and I did not know there were still outhouses in the US. We went on with our travels.

The next stop was Missouri. We were running out of money for food and lodging. As I was driving through Saint Louis, I started to act erratically. Paranoid schizophrenia had taken control of me. I shouted out the window of the car as I was weaving in and out of traffic, yelling, "Christians, turn your lights on." I wanted all the people who were Christians to turn their headlights on that way. I knew' they were people of God. I forgot to mention that I sang all the way home. My husband was so afraid that even his eyelashes turned white; he lost all color.

We finally turned into a motel, and we were totally exhausted. We didn't have enough money to pay for a room. My husband asked the lady if she could help us. She contacted a church group that helped stranded travelers. So, as luck would have it, we had a place for the night. I called my adopted mom, Ruthie, and told her where we were. She is Catholic and told me every city in Missouri was named after a saint. I also called my sister-in-law, Patricia, who was praying for us to come home; and Ruthie was praying. I was so mentally ill that I could not sleep. I sang Christian songs all night. My husband fell asleep. The next morning, we decided to drive straight through since we had very little money and nothing to eat. We were on our way to Ohio. God spoke to me and said, "You passed your brother on the way to Arizona. Do not pass him on your way home."

On the highway to Ohio, it was very dark, and there was construction at night. I could hardly see. I prayed and asked God to help me.

He said, "Sherry, I will lend you my eyes to see."

After that, I saw clearly, and we went on our way. When we got to Ohio, my husband had to go to the restroom. He told me not to get out of the car. Did I obey? No, I did not listen. I walked up to some strangers and asked if they knew who the king of the universe was?

They replied to the question, "It is the Lord Jesus."

My husband came out and yelled at me to get in the car. I told him not until my brother came. I didn't know how to get to my brother's house. I went inside and asked the cashier to talk to my brother and tell him where we were. She told him where we were. He said he would be right there. He was right around the corner, and we didn't even know how close we were to him. He was there in about five minutes or less.

He called my name and said, "It's your brother, Bill."

He told us to follow him. It was then that I got into the car. We got a shower and laid down to rest. I fell right to sleep. The next morning when we got up, my brother introduced me to my nephew, Regis. We all went out for breakfast. It was an all you-can-eat buffet. I only ate an English muffin and orange juice, even though I was very hungry.

My brother said to my husband, "My sister is not feeling well?"

My husband said, "She has not been well the whole trip."

We took a picture and got ready to go home. I looked at my hand after my brother left. He had given me a hundred dollars. That was enough to get home and then some. We were surprised. He is a nurse, and he really wanted us to get home. He knew we were both sick from stress and the trip. The next sign we saw said, "Welcome to West Virginia." I was happy that we were almost home, but in the next scenario, I started to hear voices. I could hear slaves screaming as if they were being hung and tortured. I sang as loud as I could to drown out the screams. I also drove fast to get out of that state, hoping it would stop the voices.

The next sign I saw said, "Welcome to Pennsylvania." The voices were gone, and I said, "Praise the Lord. We made it." We reached our home about two hours later because we stopped to eat. As soon as we arrived home, my husband kissed the ground. He said we'll never go that far from home again.

We immediately called our doctor and made an appointment. He told us to rest because we were physically and mentally exhausted and he would see us the next day. Upon seeing our doctor, he warned us if we did not get our proper rest we would come unglued. Ken went to bed but I could not sleep. I stayed up all night reading, singing, smoking and praying. Finally I laid down for a while and drifted off to sleep.

# My Song, Poetry and Inspiration

**Yvonne's Cadence for The Lord**

Leader says: Soldiers, are you ready?
*Answer: Whew. Ready to rock!*

Leader: We are in the Lord's Army. (Repeat)
Leader: We will fight till we are free (Repeat)
Leader: God will never let us down (Repeat)
Leader: Cause he doesn't want Satan around. (Repeat)
Leader: Knock the devil knock him out (Repeat)
Leader: Because God knows what he's all about. (Repeat)
Leader: Yvonne gonna give a smile. (Repeat)
Leader: Because she has been fighting the devil awhile. (Repeat)
Leader: Pastor King and Pastor Jo are God's girls.
Leader: We're gonna tell the whole world. (Repeat)
Leader: God will put Satan down. (Repeat)
Leader: In a hole in the ground. (Repeat)
Leader: We will bow on bended knees.
Leader: Then we all will be free.

Sound off one two Sound off three four
Sound off 1 2 3 4 1 2 3 4

## Poem for Pastor

When I see you, it makes me smile.
You have God-like ways and a special style.
You stand so tall I can see what a woman who loves God can be.
You wake up early just like me.
To spend time with God to make us free.
The words from God you speak.
It helps others reach their peak.
Your sermons are clear and precise.
Even though sometimes they cut like a knife. God told me to tell you a job well done.
He doesn't mind you having fun.
Never forget I appreciate you.
You are God's gift to me and others too.
Now we must give God all the praise for the fact he has kept us all these days.

**Never Alone**

My best friend is a spirit
I have other friends
But my spirit friend is always around
He never lets me down
He is never tired and always available
So I always have his company even when it seems I am alone
Even when it is to early to telephone
I can feel his presence in music
See his face in art
Watch his beauty in nature
Just as a plant grows so does my love for my spirit friend
Even in death our friendship cannot end.
One day I hope to behold his glorious light
I'll close my eyes in death only to awake in spirit form
to see my best friend
With his love life will never end
Oh how magnificent that will be
To behold his Holy light

**Easter is Not a Show**

This is the time of year when we get all dressed up
New shoes new outfit candy for the kids
Did we forget the true meaning of the season?
Our Savior died for our sins
Yes Jesus, died for us
He was raised from the dead and lives again
We don't need any blood sacrifices
The blood of our Savior was the perfect one
Nothing is to bad we repent and ask the Lord's forgiveness
The Lord wants us all to be saved
He is not prejudice
Thank you Lord for not judging us by the color of our skin
I praise and thank God for the gift of writing these words
So all may know
This Easter don't put on a show
Come to the Lord and he'll show you the way to go.

**I'm me**

*I'm loving life just being me*
*Lord thank you for letting me be me*
*I wouldn't want to be someone else*
*I'm doing my best to be a better me*
*Thank you lord for letting me be me*
*I pray and I hope for a change in me*
*One who walks closer to the Lord*
*You see to me, God love is Eternal*
*Thank you Lord for loving me and letting me* be me.

—Adam Dehner

www.ingramcontent.com/pod-product-compliance
Lightning Source LLC
LaVergne TN
LVHW051926060526
838201LV00062B/4711